american press
520 Commonwealth Avenue #416, Boston, Mass. 02215
thought yo

the author . . .

STEWART

William J. Stewart is an Associate Professor of Education at the University of Northern Iowa in Cedar Falls.

the book . . .

TRANSFORMING TRADITIONAL UNIT TEACHING

1st ed., May 1982, paperback text ed., perfect bound, ISBN #0-89641-107-9, list price $4.95x, trim size 5½×8½, 87 pp., shpwt. 5 oz.

This text is suitable for both undergraduate and graduate education courses. It outlines a practical, flexible plan to eliminate the disadvantages while retaining and improving the advantages of traditional unit teaching. This plan expedites and simplifies the planning, organization, management, and assessment processes of unit teaching. Basic concepts underlying unit teaching and the resource unit are examined, and the construction and application of the resource unit is described. The ways in which modified unit teaching can accommodate the various abilities, interests, and needs of the learners are outlined, along with how the modified unit teaching plan can be used to teach basic skills in addition to attitudes and understandings. How the progress of learners is determined and reported is also explained. Finally, the text specifies how pre- and in-service teacher education programs can be developed to bring about awareness, knowledge, and understanding of the modified unit teaching concept and technique. A list of selected further reading is included.

Contents: INTRODUCTION. UNIT TEACHING. THE RESOURCE UNIT: The Components of the Resource Unit. MAXIMIZING UNIT TEACHING: The Structure of the Modified Unit Teaching Plan. Actualizing the Modified Unit Teaching Plan. INDIVIDUALIZATION OF INSTRUCTION: Individual Characteristics. Individualization: The Concept and Technique. Individualization and Unit Teaching. DEVELOPING THE RESOURCE UNIT: Selecting the Resource Unit. Constructing the Resource Unit: *Identifying the Curricular Approaches. Formulating the Instructional Objectives. Designating*

(over)

the Instructional Activities. Selecting the Instructional Materials and Resources. Planning the Evaluation Devices. APPLYING THE RESOURCE UNIT: The Lesson Plan: *Selecting the Instructional Objectives. Selecting the Instructional Activities. Selecting the Instructional Materials and Resources. Selecting the Evaluation Devices.* Teacher Planning. Learner-Teacher Planning. The Planning Period. The Working Period. Flexible Grouping: *Large Group Teaching-Learning Situations. Small Group Teaching-Learning Situations. Individual Teaching-Learning Situations.* EVALUATING AND REPORTING LEARNER PROGRESS: Grading. Evaluation. Reporting Learner Progress. TEACHER EDUCATION: The Pre-Service Program: *The Pre-Service Unit Teaching Model.* The In-Service Education Program: *Resource Unit Development.* Supervision. SELECTED READINGS: Articles. Books and Booklets.

Transforming Traditional Unit Teaching

William J. Stewart
Associate Professor of Education
University of Northern Iowa

AMERICAN PRESS
Boston, Massachusetts

Printed in the United States of America.

Library of Congress Catalog Card Number: 82-71293

Contents

Introduction

Although the idea has been with us for many years, unit teaching still essentially remains a largely unfulfilled goal. In all probability, this can be primarily attributed to the fact that the unit procedure has typically been both difficult and time-consuming to apply. Consquently, *Transforming Traditional Unit Teaching* introduces a practical, flexible plan that eliminates the disadvantages, but retains and improves the advantages of traditional unit teaching. This modified format greatly expedites and simplifies the planning, organizational, management, and assessment processes of unit teaching so as to maximize its effects.

The chapters that follow present this new unit teaching approach in terms of its underlying theory, principles, meaning, characteristics, possibilities, and application. More specifically, this book

- provides a general frame of reference by examining the basic concepts that underlie both unit teaching and the resource unit;
- suggests how unit teaching can be modified to accelerate, extend, and simplify its use;
- describes how the resource unit is constructed and applied in the modified unit teaching plan;
- explains how the modified unit teaching plan organizes and unifies the learning objectives, activities, materials, and evaluation devices into a comprehensive, instructional management system;
- points out how the modified unit teaching approach effectively accommodates the various abilities, interests, and needs of the learners;

- discusses how the modified unit teaching plan can be used to teach the basic skills in addition to attitudes and understandings;
- tells how the progress of the learners is determined and reported in the modified unit teaching format;
- specifies how pre and in-service teacher education programs can be developed to bring about awareness, knowledge, and understanding of the modified unit teaching concept and technique.

Transforming Traditional Unit Teaching is suitable for use in both undergraduate and graduate education courses; in addition, it can be considered a reference book for in-service professionals.

William J. Stewart

Cedar Falls, Iowa
March, 1982

Chapter I
Unit Teaching

Classroom instruction must be well planned if it is to be interesting, relevant, and meaningful. Worthwhile instruction also necessitates that the various teaching-learning components, which include the objectives, activities, materials, and evaluation devices, be organized into an operational framework. These things can be effectively accomplished through unit teaching, because it lends direction, form, and unity to the instructional process, and translates the teaching-learning components into manageable, plausible plans.

Unit teaching can be defined as a procedure for enabling the teacher to organize, manage, and diversify teaching-learning components in accordance with the unique individual characteristics of the learners. The unit procedure offers a number of significant advantages. Specifically:

Unit teaching effectuates individualization of instruction. The unit procedure adapts instruction to the pupils' varied abilities, interests, and needs. Unit teaching makes it possible for the learners to be involved with highly diversified teaching-learning tasks. More or less uniform achievement standards give way, in the unit procedure, to widely differentiated achievement levels that conform to each learner's individual characteristics and requirements.

Unit teaching is based upon the principles of how learning actually occurs. Learning implies much more than the mere acquisition of information or the ability to do certain things. Real learning results in a behavioral change in the pupil. This indicates that the pupil assimilates specific learnings, into his or her behavioral pattern, so as to ultimately be able to apply them to the solution of academic, personal, and social problems. Unit teaching makes it possible for the pupils to be involved with learning tasks which lead to constructive and positive changes in behavior.

Unit teaching provides for a wide variety of instructional objectives, activities, materials, and evaluation devices. The unit procedure enables the teacher to match a broad selection of teaching-learning components to the individual differences of the learners. This can cause learner groupings to change, from time to time, within the classroom. At certain times, instructional situations might be developed for the total class; at other times, for small groups of learners; and, sometimes, for an individual learner.

Unit teaching enables the teacher to organize teaching-learning components into a unified whole. The unit procedure not only unifies the instructional objectives, activities, materials, and evaluation devices, but also relates fundamental knowledges to the development of attitudes, skills, and understandings. Further, unit teaching links activities in progress to previously studied activities, and to activities to be undertaken.

Unit teaching helps the pupils to learn how to cooperate and to share with others. The pupils learn how to work with other members of the group, and how to become considerate of others. Attitudes, skills, and understandings are shared; and, as a consequence, each pupil makes a contribution to the further learning of other pupils within the group.

Unit teaching incorporates the problem-solving approach. The unit procedure provides opportunities for the learners to solve realistic problems. For this purpose, unit teaching allows for the use of the problem-solving method in which the learners are able to: (1) define problems, (2) set up hypotheses, (3) collect data, (4) analyze the data, (5) draw conclusions, and (6) plan an appropriate course of action.

Unit teaching provides for the practical application of knowledges, skills, and understandings. The unit procedure makes it possible for the learners to compute, read, write, solve problems, and work with others in practical teaching-learning situations. Unit teaching correlates the instructional objectives, activities, materials, and evaluation devices with the everyday concerns, interests, and problems of the learners. This enables the learners to better appreciate and understand the relationship of school experiences to real life. In addition, the unit procedure can adapt teaching and learning to the characteristics, conditions, and resources of the community.

Unit teaching integrates the various subjects. The learners' interests and needs often make it necessary to develop teaching-learning situations that combine content items from several subjects. To this end, unit teaching can be used to consolidate the content items from more than one subject area.

Unit teaching provides for cooperative learner-teacher planning. The unit procedure makes it possible for the pupils to participate in the planning, development, and evaluation of teaching-learning situations. This enables the pupils to become involved with problems that pertain to their individual requirements; and, therefore, results in learning experiences that are purposeful, significant, and of concern to each pupil. Moreover, the pupils, through taking part in learner-teacher planning, have many opportunities to be creative, take initiative, make decisions, accept responsibility, and work and share with others.

Unit teaching provides for cooperative, comprehensive, continuous, and coordinated evaluation. The unit procedure makes it possible for evaluation to be learner-teacher planned. Unit teaching includes a wide range of evaluation devices such as: anecdotal records, autobiographies, checklists, questionnaires, sociometric tests, teacher-made tests, and work samples.

Also, in unit teaching, evaluation occurs on a continuous basis, instead of only at a terminal point, and the evaluation devices are coordinated and interrelated with the instructional objectives and activities.

Chapter II
The Resource Unit

The resource unit makes it possible for the teacher to plan, organize, manage, and evaluate large group, small group, and individual teaching-learning situations in accordance with the individual characteristics of the learners. The resource unit may be defined as a collection of many and varied instructional objectives, activities, materials, and evaluation devices organized around a specific unifying problem, theme, or topic. The resource unit may be designed for one classroom, a single grade level, or multiple grade levels. Likewise, the components, of the resource unit, may be restricted to a single subject, or they may traverse subjects.

The resource unit draws the various suggestions of teaching-learning components into a comprehensive, cohesive, coherent framework. The learners might be taught, through the resource unit's numerous suggestions of teaching-learning components, to do such things as: solve a problem, develop an idea, or become acquainted with a series of understandings.

The teacher obtains suggestions of teaching-learning components, from the resource unit, for developing specific lesson plans for one or more learners. The resource unit must be flexible and subject to revision, because the teacher, in meeting the individual differences of the learners, may have to modify or even create new teaching-learning components. Also, it is not likely that the teacher will make use of all the suggestions of teaching-learning components set down in a given resource unit.

The Components of the Resource Unit

A functional teaching-learning situation usually requires the use of many different instructional objectives, activities, materials, and evaluation devices. These various components, of the resource unit, constitute an interrelated and interdependent whole. The resource unit's components become separate items only when abstracted from the unified whole for the purpose of description and analysis. Each component, of the resource unit, is discussed below:

The Instructional Objectives. The objectives answer the question, "Why?" They serve as a means for directing and specifying teaching-learning situations. All other components, of the resource unit, are developed for the purpose of accomplishing the objectives. The resource unit contains extensive and varied suggestions of realistically attainable objectives. Every teaching-learning situation is formulated on the basis of one or more objective(s).

Provision must be made, in the resource unit, for affective, cognitive, and psychomotor objectives. Affective objectives are related to the development of attitudes, appreciations, feelings, and values. Cognitive objectives refer to the teaching of concepts, generalizations, knowledges, basic skills, and understandings. Psychomotor objectives pertain to the development of physically-oriented skills.

The Instructional Activities. The activities tell "how" the objectives are to be achieved. The resource unit usually contains a variety of activities, for each objective, so as to accommodate the individual characteristics of the learners. There might also be cases in which the same or a similar activity is indicated for more than one objective.

The activities may be classified as introductory, developmental, and culminating. Introductory activities are designed to stimulate interest in, and to create an awareness of a problem or topic. These activities might include: dramatizations, field trips, films, and textbook readings. Developmental activities comprise the on-going work of the learners. These activities might include: conducting interviews, constructing charts and graphs, and writing stories, plays, and poems. Culminating activities are used to bring learning experiences to a conclusion. These activities might include: conducting review discussions, making reports, and presenting displays.

The Instructional Materials and Resources. The materials and resources tell "with what" the objectives can be achieved, and are designated for each activity. The materials and resources might include such aids as: books, magazines, pamphlets, films, filmstrips, and community resources.

The Evaluation Devices. The evaluation devices tell "how well" the objectives have been achieved, and are based directly on them. Evaluation devices are used for assessing such learning behaviors as: attitudes, skills, and understandings. Some examples of evaluation devices are: work samples, checklists, rating scales, tests, conferences, and written summaries.

Chapter III
Maximizing Unit Teaching

Certain factors have tended to severely limit the impact of traditional unit teaching. First, the development of overly complex resource units has required an inordinate amount of teacher planning time. Second, the unwieldy form and structure of these units have made it difficult for teachers to be able to quickly translate suggestions of instructional objectives, activities, materials, and evaluation devices into actual teaching-learning situations. Third, unit teaching has not typically been applied to organize, unify, and manage the total array of classroom methods, materials, and resources. Finally, unit teaching has not been used, to a substantial and pervasive degree, in all subjects at all grade levels. Therefore, these various factors signal the need to modify unit teaching in order to accelerate, extend, and simplify its use.

This chapter sets forth a plan which modifies unit teaching, so as to enable teachers to obtain the maximum results from its use. To this end, the following pages: (1) explain the structure of the modified unit teaching plan, (2) define its terms, (3) delineate its concepts, and (4) present the strategies for implementing it.

The Structure of the Modified Unit Teaching Plan

The diagram, that appears on the following page, identifies the various items that constitute the modified unit teaching plan. This diagram also illustrates the

The Modified Unit Teaching Plan

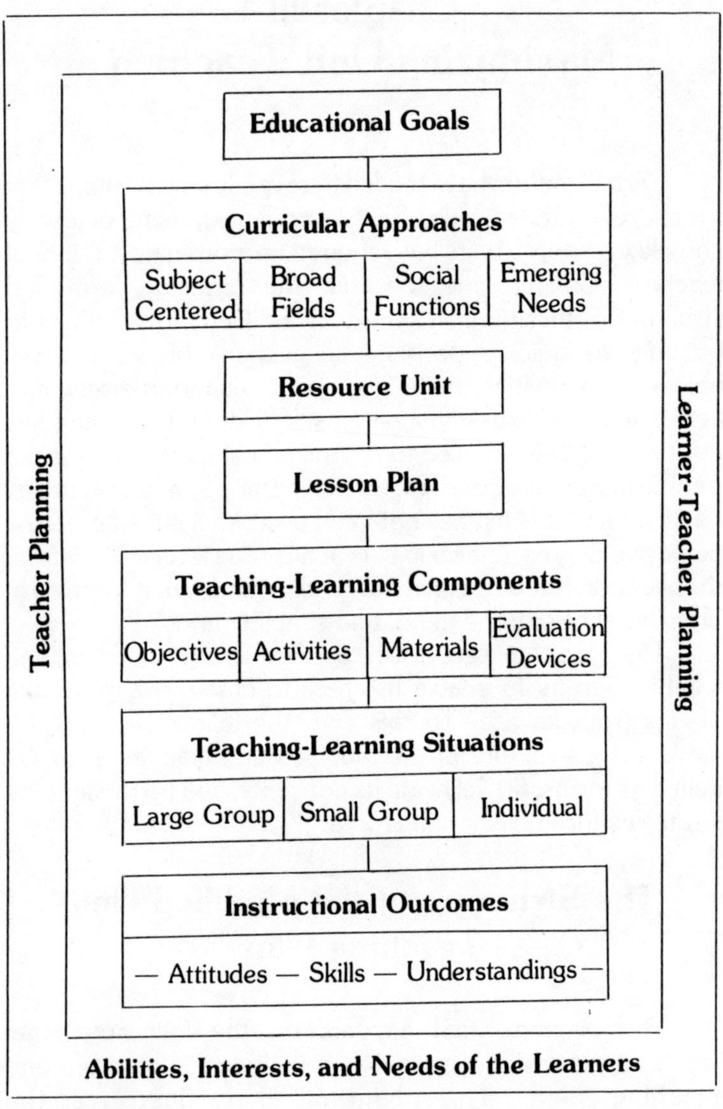

interrelationships of these items. These items and relations, which are briefly explained in this section, are further detailed elsewhere in this book.

Teaching Planning; Learner-Teacher Planning; and the Abilities, Interests, and Needs of the Learners. The placement of these items on the perimeters of the diagram is meant to show that they permeate all other items and steps in the diagram.

The Educational Goals. These refer to the overall educational aims or purposes which might be sought on a local, regional, state, or national basis. The educational goals provide direction for what is ultimately taught and learned in the classroom.

The Subject Curricular Approach. This approach is based upon the separate subjects. The major emphasis, in the subject approach, is on the acquisition of facts and information, and there can, also, be much reliance on repetitive drill.

The Broad Fields Curricular Approach. This approach is focused upon a combination of subjects arranged into a broad field such as language arts or social studies. The broad fields approach, like the subject approach, features content acquisition.

The Major Social Functions Curricular Approach. This approach is centered on the basic functions or activities of society that are common to all individuals. For example, all people need to communicate, to have recreation or to use their leisure time wisely, to become familiar with and use various means of transportation, and to conserve human and natural resources. Thus, instruction, in this approach, is organized around these common social functions. Formal subject lines are eliminated since the social functions and processes cut across the various fields of knowledge. Also, problem-solving techniques are commonly used in this approach.

The Emerging Needs Curricular Approach. This approach is concerned with the emerging personal needs of the learners. In this approach, content is drawn from the various subjects as needed. The emerging needs are related to such behaviors as: attitudes, self-expectations, and how the learners feel about themselves.

The Resource Unit. The resource unit is a file of suggestions of instructional objectives, activities, materials, and evaluation devices organized around a specific unifying theme or problem. The resource unit functions as a reference for enabling the teacher to plan, organize, and manage diversified teaching-learning components, in relation to the above-mentioned curricular approaches, for both individual and group situations. In essence, the resource unit serves as a blueprint for helping the teacher to make the best use of teaching-learning components.

The resource unit is not designed to be taught as developed; but, rather, to serve as a "resource." It would neither be desirable nor possible to use, with any one learner or group of learners, all of the teaching-learning components contained in a given resource unit.

The Lesson Plan. The lesson plan, which is drawn from the resource unit, functions as the vehicle through which specific suggestions of instructional objectives, activities, materials, and evaluation devices are planned for and with the learners. In the modified unit teaching plan, the suggestions of teaching-learning components, contained in the lesson plan, can be in either numerical or statement form. However, in all probability, the numerical format would be most commonly used, because it can best enable the teacher to quickly convert suggestions of teaching-learning components into actual instructional situations.

The Instructional Objectives. The objectives refer to what is expected to be accomplished or the anticipated outcomes.

The Instructional Activities. The activities serve as the means by which the instructional objectives are to be achieved.

The Instructional Materials. The materials are used to carry out the instructional activities.

The Evaluation Devices. The function of the evaluation devices is to determine the extent and nature of the learners' progress toward accomplishing the instructional objectives.

Large Group, Small Group, and Individual Teaching-Learning Situations. These various types of teaching-learning situations are appropriately formed in accordance with the characteristics and objectives of the learners. In flexible grouping, the individual objectives of the learners might take precedence over those of the group. Thus, the objectives would first be determined for and with each learner; and, then, subsequent large group and small group situations would be comprised of those learners who share similar objectives.

Instructional Outcomes. These refer to the attitudes, skills, and understandings that are sought through the use of a particular resource unit. Attitudes include appreciations, interests, and values to be developed; skills include specific actions or habits to be fostered; and understandings include concepts, facts, generalizations, principles, and rules.

Actualizing the Modified Unit Teaching Plan

The following paragraphs consider the various factors involved in the actualization of the modified unit teaching plan. Specifically:

The modified unit teaching plan results in a total instructional management system. Heretofore, unit teaching has typically been used to merely reinforce and supplement such teaching-learning techniques as the textbook, programmed learning, and computer assisted instruction. Whereas, the modified unit teaching format represents a highly centralized means for organizing and integrating all learning objectives, methods of presentation, materials, and evaluation devices into a comprehensive, coherent, and cohesive instructional management system.

The modified unit teaching plan includes all subjects at all grade levels. Unit teaching has traditionally been restricted almost exclusively to elementary school social studies. In actuality, however, all subjects embody instructional objectives, activities, materials, and evaluation devices. Thus, the modified unit teaching approach, with its capability to incorporate teaching-learning components into a total instructional management system, can be adapted to all subjects at all grade levels.

The modified unit teaching plan features a simplified resource unit. Resource units have typically included: extensive and detailed introductory statements; unnecessary lists of content items; indistinct, rambling statements of activities; and overly elaborate motivational and concluding activities. Obviously, these things have tended to greatly reduce the resource unit's effectiveness and efficiency. On the other hand, the more simplified resource unit, in the modified unit teaching plan, presents, in clear and concise terms, only those components which are absolutely necessary for the creation of functional teaching-learning situations. These include the instructional objectives, activities, materials, and evaluation devices.

The modified unit teaching plan relates the resource unit directly to the lesson plan; and, thereby, eliminates the teaching unit. In traditional unit teaching, the teaching unit is drawn from the resource unit, and the lesson plan, in turn, is derived from the teaching unit. However, it has been very time-consuming for the teacher to have to make decisions about which suggetions of teaching-learning components to select from the resource unit; and, then, to have to copy the statements of these suggestions into the teaching unit. This is further complicated by the fact that teaching units have almost invariably contained many more suggestions than could actually be used.

The teaching unit is eliminated, in the modified unit teaching plan, because it does not serve any purpose that cannot be accomplished by the lesson plan. Therefore, the teacher develops the lesson plan directly from the resource unit. This lesson plan contains only the approximate number of suggestions of teaching-learning components to be actually used. It also indicates these suggestions in the form of either numbers or statements.

The modified unit teaching plan provides for the use of the random and/or developmental instructional design(s). In the random design, the objectives and activities, contained in the resource unit and/or lesson plan, are arranged in preferred order, but independent of each other, so that they can be taught and learned in nonsequential fashion. Whereas, in the more directed and systematized developmental design, the objectives and activities are organized into a relatively tight prioritized series in which the mastery of one learning task is required as a prerequisite to beginning another task. This planned sequence results in teaching and learning that occurs on a step-by-step basis. Essentially, the developmental design begins at a simple, elementary stage and moves progressively toward the more complex. In addition, there might be instances in which it would be desirable to combine various elements from both the random and developmental designs in a particular resource unit and/or lesson plan.

The modified unit teaching plan accommodates not only the teaching of attitudes and understandings, but the basic skills as well. Unit teaching has typically been confined to the use of the random instructional design. This design is particularly well adapted to the teaching of attitudes and understandings. However, as mentioned above, the modified unit teaching plan can also include the developmental instructional design which is especially useful for teaching the basic arithmetic, reading, and writing skills.

The modified unit teaching plan provides for the use of the index card resource unit. The traditional resource unit, in the form of a bound document, has proven to be too complex and unmanageable. Therefore, the modified unit teaching plan advocates the index card-file for organizing and managing the resource unit.

The index card resource unit greatly accelerates and simplifies unit teaching, because it makes it possible for the teacher and learners to quickly flip to the precise location of a desired card; and, then, to pull it for immediate use. This card-file also makes it easy to add new suggestions of teaching-learning components, and to remove others if they do not prove to be useful.

Each index card, of the resource unit, indicates an objective and a related activity on its obverse side. (See Figure 1.) The corresponding materials and evaluation devices are designated on the reverse side of the card. (See Figure 2.) The obverse side of the sample card, shown in Figure 1, is also numbered in the upper right-hand corner. The purpose of this number is to make it easier to locate the card in the resource unit file; and, then, to key it to the lesson plan.

Topic: "The American Revolution" No. 1

Objective

To teach the important role of women during the American Revolution so that the learners will be aware of many of the heroic deeds performed by women during the war.

Activity

After viewing the filmstrip, "The Revolution: Women in the American Revolution, Legend and Reality" the learners will discuss women's various individual contributions to the war effort.[1]

Figure 1

[1]Jean Mahoney, *The American Revolution*. Prepared for Principles of Teaching K-6, Westfield State College, Westfield, Mass., p. 17.

"The American Revolution"

Materials

Filmstrip—"The Revolution: Women in the American Revolution, Legend and Reality," Listening Library, Inc., Old Greenwich, Conn., 1978.

Book-Clyne, Patricia Edwards, *Patriots in Petticoats.* New York: Dodd, Mead, and Co., 1976.

Evaluation

Each learner will draw a picture, depicting an incident experienced by one of the mentioned heroines; and, then, will explain the picture to the total class.[1]

Figure 2

The modified unit teaching plan provides for the use of computerized resource units. Computer technology can be applied to make unit teaching more effective and efficient. The computer can, within a matter of minutes, retrieve, generate, and print suggestions of objectives, activities, materials, and evaluation devices matched to the decisions that the teacher makes about the various abilities, interests, and needs of the learners.

[1]*Ibid.*, pp. 17, 30, 33.

Computerized unit teaching offers many significant advantages. To be specific, when computer technology is applied to unit teaching it becomes possible:

- to provide teachers with immediate access to a resource unit in a computer located many miles away;
- for teachers to quickly match teaching-learning components to the characteristics and requirements of the learners;
- to save teachers much valuable planning time, since the computer can quickly process instructional decisions;
- for the teacher to readily add, delete, or modify the teaching-learning components of the resource unit;
- for teachers to share and use resource units not only within their own school systems, but on a regional, state, and national basis as well.

The computerized resource unit contains suggestions of teaching-learning components that have been coded to such learner variables as interests and reading level. The teacher, in making use of the computerized unit, initially makes decisions concerning the characteristics and objectives of the learners.

These decisions are then fed into the computer, which, in turn, retrieves appropriate suggestions of teaching-learning components from a computerized resource unit. Next, the computer generates and prints a lesson plan that contains various suggestions of activities, materials, and evaluation devices per each objective for the total class, a small group, or an individual learner.

The suggestions of teaching-learning components, contained in the computerized resource unit, must be used in a flexible, selective fashion. This means that teachers need to thoroughly understand unit teaching, and be experienced in using it, before attempting to make use of computerized unit teaching. The teacher must also have much expertise in knowing how to either modify or create new teaching-learning components in accordance with the abilities, interests, and needs of the learners.

Computer technology can also be applied to enable state education departments to quickly disseminate the contents of curriculum guides to school districts. This is very significant in view of the fact that the production and distribution of such guides has traditionally been an important function of state education agencies. Putting resource units into computers can enable a state group to immediately share its guides with school district professionals, who can then modify the guides in any way they like. Thus, the curriculum guides, under a state education department's own imprint, would be both similar and different. Furthermore, computer technology can enable state education agencies to cut costs on the production and distribution of curriculum guides, because the desktop microcomputer, with its video display screen for viewing the contents of the guides, eliminates the high cost of setting up print and using paper.

Chapter IV
Individualization of Instruction

Individualization of instruction signifies the adaption of teaching-learning situations to the unique individual characteristics of each learner. Unit teaching engenders individualization of instruction, because it enables the teacher to incorporate widely diversified instructional objectives, activities, materials, and evaluation devices into individualized teaching-learning situations. The teacher, in order to successfully effectuate individualization of instruction through unit teaching, must first take the individual characteristics of each learner into account; and, then, develop appropriate individualized teaching-learning situations to accommodate these characteristics.

Individual Characteristics

Chronological age is not a satisfactory measure of the developmental level of a learner. To say that a learner is ten years old is to say no more than that learner has lived ten years. In actual development, this learner may be equal to the average twelve-year-old, or the average eight-year-old. But even to say that this learner is advanced, or normal, or slow in development is an over-simplification. Each learner is, in a sense, a complex of several beings: a physical being, an intellectual being, a social being, and so on. In growing, a learner does not advance evenly in all of the several aspects that make up the total self. The learner may be advanced in some areas of growth and slow in others. As Goodlad wrote:

> Viewing man as a class of creatures, one is struck with the overriding common features shared by all members of the species. Viewing a group of men brought together for a common purpose, one is struck by the startling person to person differences that make agreement on even the nature of the purpose difficult. They are the differences that complicate the problems of schoolkeeping.[1]

It logically follows that there will be great differences between and among the learners in any classroom. If they are grouped, on the basis of chronological age, there may be wide differences in the levels of emotional, mental, physical, and social maturity. If the learners are grouped, on the basis of achievement level, they may vary widely in chronological age with corresponding differences in social and emotional maturity and in capacity to grow. Also, when the learners are grouped, according to level of achievement, their equality, with reference to this criterion, is only partial and temporary. The learners do not achieve equally in all the subject areas of the curriculum. They may be average with respect to some, slow or accelerated with respect to others. Moreover, they grow toward maturity at different rates, and each learner has a highly individualized pattern of growth. Some grow at an even tempo; some start slowly and increase the tempo later; others start fast, then slow down. If ever it were possible to get together, at a given time, a group of learners, all of equal achievement, the passage of only a few months would be

---

[1]John I. Goodlad, *School, Curriculum, and the Individual.* Waltham, Mass.: Blaisdell Pub. Co., 1966, p. 5.

necessary for noticeable differences to develop. Teachers, however, should seek to accommodate these individual differences, not to eliminate them. In line with this, Herrick et al. observed that:

> There is no method of grouping, teaching, or classifying children which will eliminate the individuality or variation that exists among and within children. Actually, to do so would prevent distinctive personality development. Differentiation in development is a prized resource to be conserved and exploited not something to be denied and destroyed.[1]

There is no measure, or combination of measures, that will bring learners into the classroom who are at the same stage of maturity in all phases of growth, who have the same capacity for growth, and who are growing at the same rate. The teacher must accept these differences and work with them. This means that the teacher must take the learners from where they are, instead of from any predetermined point, established by norms or averages, and guide their total growth in desirable directions as fast and as far as they can go.

The teacher, so as to effectively provide for individual differences, must know each learner's stage of development and growth potential, must select materials for instruction that are appropriate for the individual learner, and must organize instructional activities so that the learners are doing what they need to do at a level where they can achieve success.

The teacher must often organize the learners into groups for effective instruction. Grouping aims to place each learner

---

[1]Virgil E. Herrick, John I. Goodlad, Frank J. Estvan, and Paul W. Eberman, *The Elementary School*. Englewood Cliffs, N.J.: Prentice-Hall, Inc., 1956, p. 103.

in a position of maximum advantage for learning. Grouping is flexible in that the learners are moved from one group to another whenever a change is necessary; a learner may be a member of one group for a given activity, of another group for a different activity. Some groups may be homogeneous with respect to ability. Other groups may be heterogeneous as to ability, but made up, for example, of learners with a common social need. Groups may be organized according to the special interests or desires of learners. Groups are guided skillfully by the teacher and disbanded when a task is completed or when interest lags.

Essentially, the teacher must accept individual characteristics as an inevitable condition of the classroom, and must not only respect these characteristics, but must make provision for them as well. In meeting individual characteristics, the teacher must know each learner's unique abilities, aspirations, and interests. Building on this knowledge, the teacher can then formulate suitable, teaching-learning situations for each learner.

Individualization: The Concept and Technique

Teaching-learning situations, which effectively accommodate the individual characteristics of the learners, consist of instructional objectives, activities, materials, and evaluation devices that are differentiated in accordance with the unique characteristics and requirements of each learner. This can be achieved through individualization of instruction, because it enables the teacher to use the individual characteristics of the learners to structure individualized teaching-learning situations.

Individualization of instruction occurs when the teaching-learning components are adapted to the unique characteristics of each learner. Both individual and group instruction are used at appropriate times, since the learner is regarded not only as an individual, but as a member of the group as well. Thus, individualization of instruction is not limited to just "individual teaching" or tutoring. Doll and Dehan pointed out that:

- in individualizing teaching, the emphasis is on the pupil as a person, the teacher as a person, and the interaction that takes place between them.
- individualization occurs when a teacher recognizes and responds to the emotional reactions of the learner as well as to his academic achievement, his intellectual mistakes, or mental deficiencies.
- individualization occurs when the teacher goes beyond ordinary achievement.
- individualization also occurs when the teacher considers the pupil to be an individual with unique perceptions, values, concepts, and needs.
- individualization is meant to lead to commitment and purpose, to sensitivity to others' needs, to awareness of the demands of truth and justice.[1]

In individualization of instruction, the objectives, for an individual learner, take precedence over those of the group. The focus is on instructional activities for individual learners with related small group and large group work whenever necessary. Clymer and Kearney listed some factors which the teacher must recognize if individualization of instruction is to be truly effective:

---

[1]Robert F. DeHaan and Ronald G. Doll, "Individualization and Human Potential," *Individualizing Instruction*. 1964 Yearbook for the Association for Supervision and Curriculum Development, Washington, D.C.: National Education Association, 1964, pp. 18-20.

- The need to know all students.
- The need to provide generous time allotments.
- The need to plan carefully whatever is to be done in the classroom.
- The need to recognize that not all teachers will adjust to individual differences in the same way.
- The need to work effectively with the group as a whole.
- The need to move slowly into any type of adjustment to individual differences.
- The need to accept more noise and confusion.
- To need to recognize failure and begin again.
- The need to accept less than 100 percent adjustment to individual differences.
- The need to recognize that adjusting to individual differences calls for plain, hard work.[1]

Individualization of instruction usually consists of five basic steps for constructing teaching-learning situations which conform to the individual characteristics of the learners. These steps denote that:

(1) the teacher must carefully assess each learner's abilities, characteristics, interests, and needs;

(2) the instructional objectives should be defined for and with each individual learner;

(3) appropriate instructional activities, materials, and evaluation devices are selected per each learner per each objective;

(4) large group, small group, and individual teaching-learning situations are appropriately developed in accordance with those learners who happen to share the same instructional objectives;

---

[1]Theodore Clymer and Nolan C. Kearney, "Curricular and Instructional Differences," *Individualizing Instruction*. The Sixty-first Yearbook of the National Society for the Study of Education, Part I, Chicago: The University of Chicago Press, 1962, p. 276.

(5) appropriate evaluation devices are used to determine the extent and nature of each learner's progress toward achieving the instructional objectives.

Individualization and Unit Teaching

The only feasible way to actualize individualization of instruction is to plan, organize, and use a wide variety of instructional objectives, activities, materials, and evaluation devices that are well suited to the individual characteristics of the learners.

Unit teaching encourages and aids individualization of instruction, because it enables the teacher to:

- determine and provide for each learner's abilities, interests, and needs;
- have access to a wide selection of instructional objectives, activities, materials, and evaluation devices for meeting each learner's characteristics and requirements;
- adapt teaching-learning components to the individual differences of the learners;
- develop appropriate large group, small group, and individual teaching-learning situations;
- make use of learner-teacher planning procedures, so that the actual interests and needs of the learners can be taken into account;
- involve the learners with independent study projects. In unit teaching, the teacher can create teaching-learning situations in terms of each learner's characteristics and requirements; and, in this way, can accommodate the full range of individual characteristics within the group.

Through unit teaching, the teacher can use teaching-learning components, of all types and all levels of difficulty, with small groups and individuals, as well as with the class as a whole. Consequently, enrichment, for the more able learners, can be achieved by selecting and assigning more challenging learning tasks, while provision may be made, for the slower progress of other learners, by selecting learning tasks at a lower level of difficulty.

Chapter V
Developing the Resource Unit

Planning is essential to the development of a good resource unit. For only through careful planning, can a unit be developed which effectively accommodates the various abilities, interests, and needs of the learners. The development of the resource unit should result in the creation of a comprehensive, yet flexible, unit which meets the demands of both individual and group instructional situations.

Resource unit development lays the foundation for actual teaching and learning. The unit should not be intended to impose a definite plan upon the learners. Instead, the suggestions of teaching-learning components, embodied in the unit, should always be regarded as tentative. In this way, the teacher and class can take advantage of any learning experiences which may happen to arise unexpectedly.

Selecting the Resource Unit

Procedures, for specifying resource units, can vary from school system to school system. In some systems, a course of study outline might signify the particular units to be used. In other systems, specific themes, or topics for units, might not be indicated. Instead the broad area, within which units are to be developed, is designated. In some systems, the teachers, themselves, have the freedom to select their own topics for units. Whatever the case, however, teachers should try to adhere to certain general standards when selecting resource units. These standards are set forth below:

- Whenever possible, the resource unit should grow out of the learner's actual interests. Typically, the teacher strives to motivate the learners to become interested in the objectives and activities of the unit. This is most likely to happen when these components are related to the natural inclinations and interests of the learners.
- The teacher must be thoroughly knowledgeable concerning the abilities, interests, and needs of the learners. Evaluation devices can provide the teacher with specific information about such variables as: emotional status, intellectual capacity, school achievement, and social maturity.
- The resource unit should provide for the continuity of learning experiences. This means that previous learnings should be used to motivate the learners to acquire new attitudes, skills, understandings, and to carry out new learning tasks.
- There should be sufficient instructional materials and resources available for developing the resource unit. The teacher must have access to a wide range of printed and illustrated materials, visual aids, community resources, and materials for art and construction activities. This is not meant to imply that expensive equipment and materials are always required, but it does mean that the teacher should have ingenuity, and be able to identify and assess what materials and resources may be available.
- The resource unit should have the capability to organize and unify all teaching-learning techniques, such as closed circuit television, programmed instruction, and the textbook, into a continuous, interacting whole.
- The resource unit should be designed to provide opportunities for learner-teacher planning and evaluation. This means that the learners should be involved in designing a proposed plan of action, putting the plan into effect, and evaluating the outcomes.

• The resource unit should provide for the development of attitudes, skills, and understandings.

Constructing the Resource Unit

The teacher, in constructing the resource unit, should seek to ensure that the unit is characterized by:

• a flexible, logical, and streamlined organizational structure;
• a readily discernable design;
• appropriate, balanced, and relevation components;
• components that are stated in clear, concise, and specific terms;
• interlocking components.

The following steps are involved in the construction of the resource unit:

(1) identifying the appropriate curricular approaches;
(2) formulating the instructional objectives in terms of the contribution that the unit can make to each learner's affective, cognitive, and psychomotor growth and development;
(3) designating those instructional activities which can most effectively contribute to the attainment of the objectives;
(4) selecting those particular instructional materials and resources that are best suited to carrying out the activities;
(5) planning ways in which the extent and nature of each learner's progress can be best evaluated.

Each of the above-mentioned steps is outlined in the sections below:

Identifying the Curricular Approaches

Once the decision has been made, concerning the selection of a particular resource unit, the teacher is ready to consider which curricular approach(es) will be used. Usually, elements, from more than one approach, will be included in a given resource unit. Each of the four basic curricular approaches is set forth below:

The Subject Centered Curricular Approach. In this approach, content is acquired within a single subject. The content follows the logical order of the particular subject. The objectives for the subject are expressed in terms of understandings to be learned and ways of thinking to be mastered. It is possible that there will be some learner-teacher planning in the subject approach, but the bulk of the planning is done by the teacher.

The Broad Fields Curricular Approach. This approach emphasizes the acquisition of content from two or more combined subjects. General science, language arts, and social studies are examples of the broad fields approach. The broad fields plan of organization permits greater freedom to use learner and community concerns and interests than the subject approach does, but still limits that use to a basic content orientation. The broad fields approach makes it possible for the pupils to be involved in selecting, organizing, carrying out, and evaluating learning experiences. However, this is still preceded by considerable teacher preplanning.

The Major Social Functions Curricular Approach. The basic orientation to this approach is in relation to the major social functions of society—the things all people, wherever they might live, have to do in order to get along. This approach expands the breadth and depth of the learners' insights into the major social functions, and increases their competence in performing these functions. Some examples of major social functions include:

becoming familiar with laws that must be obeyed;

being willing to contribute individual abilities for the good of the group;

taking part in selecting classmates for various responsibilities;

learning to give and take in relation to others.

The basic assumption, underlying the major social functions approach, denotes that the learners must be involved in the planning. Pupil-teacher planning goes on as a part of the learning experiences. However, teacher preplanning also precedes the learners' involvement in the planning process. In most schools, the social studies program is about the only area doing very much with the major social functions approach as an organizational framework. Another area has been health and to some extent science.

The Emerging Needs Curricular Approach. This approach deals with the emerging personal needs of the learners, and what is required to meet these needs. The emerging needs approach pertains to identifying, defining, and meeting the needs of the learners within the context of their day-to-day living. The scope of the curriculum is the scope of the learner at any given time, and it will broaden and deepen as rapidly as the learner's world expands. The teacher and the learners are the major planning unit in the emerging needs approach. Planning is a continuous examination and study of ongoing experiences—in order to determine content, processes, and to clarify next steps. Planning is an integral part of learning in this approach. Some examples of emerging needs include:

learning how to express anger without hurting self or others;

knowing how to cope with fear or worry;

knowing when to express and when to suppress emotions;

recognizing how attitudes and values affect the decisions that one makes;

gaining realistic insight into one's personal strengths and weaknesses.

Formulating the Instructional Objectives

After taking the curricular approaches into consideration, the teacher is in a position to develop the instructional objectives. The more carefully teachers think through the objectives the better prepared they are to recognize, and to pick up leads from the learners, and to guide their thinking. In addition, teachers must be ready to adjust or change objectives as actual teaching-learning situations evolve, and more worthwhile possibilities appear.

The resource unit contains specific statements of objectives, pertaining to various attitudes, skills, and understandings, which might be developd through the application of the unit. The objectives are intended to be used for the teacher's preplanning; and, therefore, should be regarded as suggestions rather than requirements.

The objectives should be stated as specific learner behaviors, since the learner is the focal point in the teaching-learning process. The objectives should also be related, on the basis of each learner's abilities, interests, and needs, directly to the selection of instructional activities, materials, and evaluation devices.

The resource unit includes many more suggestions of objectives than can possibly be used in any one lesson plan. This better enables the teacher to adjust the lesson plan to fit specific individual and group teaching-learning situations. However, the list of objectives should be limited to only attainable, relevant objectives, so that it won't become so long that it cannot be easily used. Moreover, this allows the objectives to function as a check for determining the adequacy of other teaching-learning components. As a result, improbable or unrealistic objectives, which cannot be used or for which no instructional activities or materials are available, can be easily eliminated.

The objecives, contained in the resource unit, can be organized into either a random instructional design or into a developmental design. Both of these instructional designs can be applied to the teaching of attitudes, skills, and understandings. However, the random design is especially useful for the teaching of attitudes and understandings, whereas, the developmental design is better suited to the teaching of skills.

In the random design, the objectives are arranged independently of each other, so that they are taught and learned in more or less nonsequential order. On the other hand, in the developmental design, the objectives are organized into a structured, systematic continuum, beginning with the most elementary objectives and progressing to the most difficult, so that they are taught and learned in a relatively tight sequential series.

The resource unit, in order to effectively provide for each learner's total development, must contain a sufficient array of affective, cognitive, and psychomotor objectives. Examples of these types of objectives follow:

AFFFECTIVE OBJECTIVES

To teach what independence means so that each learner will be able to arrive at personal conclusions and act in ways that are personally satisfying but not detrimental to the welfare of others.

To teach what a leader is so that each learner will be able to demonstrate his or her personal leadership qualities.

COGNITIVE OBJECTIVES

To teach the lifestyle of a patriotic family during the American Revolution so that the learners will be able to relate the changes brought to everyday life by war.

To teach the events which led the colonies into the Revolution so that the learners will know how the war actually began.

PSYCHOMOTOR OBJECTIVES

To teach the role of the American Navy during the Revolutionary War so that the learners can construct models of the vessels of the day.

To teach military drill practices so that the learners will be able to demonstrate the drills used by various foreigners during the Revolutionary War.[1]

Suggestions of instructional objectives can be obtained from such sources as: curriculum guides, professional journals, and textbooks. Teachers, through engaging in the study, discussion, and critical evaluation of statements of objectives, can learn much about how to develop and to maintain balance between and among affective, cognitive, and psychomotor objectives.

Following are general guidelines for writing objectives:

- Each objective should be stated in terms which call for the performance of a specific behavioral task such as: analyzing, applying, comparing, identifying, listing, or making.
- Each objective should be capable of being evaluated. This means that the objective should be related to the appropriate evaluation device(s).
- Each objective should require the performance of a specific learning task by the pupil.

---

[1]Mahoney, *op. cit.*, pp. 12, 13, 14, 15, 19, 22.

• Each objective should require a single learner behavior so as to minimize confusion in the evaluation procedures. For if a particular objective calls for multiple learner behaviors, it will then be necessary that there be more than one interpretation for the evaluation of that objective.

• Each objective should be flexible. If the objective is stated too specifically the teaching-learning components, designated for use with that objective, will be too limited; and, therefore, will not permit the number of approaches necessary for accommodating the individual differences of the learners.

Designating the Instructional Activities

The instructional activities are the means through which the learners are able to achieve the objectives. The activities should be suggestions which are best suited to the attainment of the objectives. The resource unit might contain activities which involve such behaviors as: experimenting, going on an excursion, arranging exhibits, taking notes, looking up references, or preparing and presenting programs.

The activities are used to: (1) stimulate interest on the part of the learners; (2) identify, collect, classify, and report information; (3) provide for the individual differences of the learners; and (4) specify ways in which the attitudes, skills, and understandings, which evolve from the study of the resource unit, may be usefully applied.

The activities may vary, from learner to learner, depending upon each learner's abilities, interests, and needs. As with the objectives, the activities can be arranged, within the resource unit, into a random instructional design, in which they are taught nonsequentially, or they can be arranged into a developmental design in which they are taught in consecutive order.

Basically, the activities contribute to the attainment of the objectives. The teacher, in selecting and planning the activities, might consider the questions listed below:

• Will the activity contribute to the expected outcomes of the resource unit?

• Will the activity be challenging and interesting to the learners?

• Will the activity provide for a variety of learning experiences?

• Is the activity within the range of accomplishment of the learners at their present stage of maturation?

Following are general criteria which teachers should consider when writing statements of activities:

• The activities should be stated in clear, concise terms so that both the teacher and the learner have a thorough knowledge and understanding of exactly what is to be achieved.

• More activities should be included than the learners are likely to actually be involved with. Then, from the activities suggested, the most appropriate ones may be selected. The teacher and learners may also add others through cooperative planning.

• There should be a balanced array of activities in any given resource unit.

• The activities should be developed in reference to: the objectives and evaluation devices contained in the resource unit; the abilities, interests, and needs of the learners; and the available materials and resources.

• The resource unit should contain extensive and varied suggestions of activities which effectively accommodate the individual differences of the learners.

• The resource unit should provide the teacher with the flexibility to add, delete, or modify activities in accordance with the requirements of the learners.

• The activities should be made interesting and meaningful enough to motivate the learners to want to pursue them.

• The activities should enable the learners to be involved in realistic teaching-learning situations, rather than in contrived settings that have no applicability outside the classroom.

• The activities should be feasible in terms of the capabilities of the learners, the availability of time, and the accessibility of instructional materials and resources.

The resource unit should contain a sufficient array of introductory, developmental, and culminating activities. It should also be recognized that there may be cases in which a particular activity may be applicable to more than one of these categories. Following are examples of the basic types of activities:

INTRODUCTORY ACTIVITIES

After viewing the filmstrip, "The American Revolution: Two Views" the learners will construct a wall chart showing the situation from both sides, British and American. The chart will contain opposing viewpoints, values, and actual numbers of men, guns, ships, etc.

After viewing the filmstrip, "Background to the American Revolution," the learners will discuss the various laws which England placed on the colonies that made the patriots feel that independence was essential. Each learner will prepare at least one document stating the law or act with an explanation of it in the style that England might have sent to and posted in the colonies.

DEVELOPMENTAL ACTIVITIES

The pupils may wish to learn Longfellow's poem, "Paul Revere's Ride" and recite it to the class. The presentation could include dramatic movements and gestures to demonstrate the furor of activity that was actually taking place and to set the mood of the night.

The pupils may wish to research just who some of the members of the Second Continental Congress were and how they came to be representatives. The report could include at least three representatives, their place of residence, and their standing in the community.

CULMINATING ACTIVITIES

The pupils may wish to learn more about the role of the Whaleboat Warriors, in the American Revolutionary War; and, then, construct a model of one that might have played a part. The Whaler should be an authentic replica of that of the Revolutionary Period, including the broad beams, shallow draft, and swivel gun.

The pupils may wish to produce the front page of a newspaper which might have come out on April 20, 1775 recounting the events of the preceding months which led to "yesterday's" outbreak at the bridge between Concord and Lexington. The frontpiece might include the famous ride of Revere, activities of the Sons of Liberty, the preparation of the minutemen, and the convincing writings of Thomas Paine.[1]

Selecting the Instructional Materials and Resources

The teacher should always be on the lookout for instructional materials and resources which will make teaching-learning situations more interesting and meaningful. What are some questions that the teacher should consider in identifying, selecting, and organizing materials and resources? First, the teacher might think about the question of relevancy; that is, whether or not the material or resource is relevant in terms of the objectives and activities? Second, is the material or resource appropriate for the learners? Third, is the material

[1] *Ibid.*, pp. 12, 13, 18, 19, 20.

or resource usable—that is, will it be available when it is needed? Fourth, is the information, which the material or resource gives, accurate?

The search for instructional materials and resources can be greatly aided if they are classified in some manner. One of the ways in which this can be done is to base the classifications on the form in which the materials and resources are available. They might be broken down into printed materials, audio-visual materials, human resources, and environmental resources.

Printed Materials. These include: textbooks, newspapers and magazines, free and inexpensive materials, reference books, school library materials, study guides, workbooks, and testing materials.

Audio-Visual Materials. These include: pictures, slides and filmstrips, exhibit pieces, films, radio and television programs, cassette recordings, maps, globes, and charts.

Human Resources. These include: the teacher who after all is the most important source of help to the learner; the learners who provide an important source of facts and information; the librarian and other members of the school staff, including both professional and service personnel; and the parents and others in the community.

Environmental Resources. These include: communication and transportation firms, business and industrial firms, museums and parks, and governmental agencies.

Instructional materials and resources are of no value if they are not in a form to be used. Therefore, it is important to organize them in such a way that maximum value can be derived from their use. Materials and resources can be organized in the following ways:

Resource Files. These are files in which materials and resources, related to various subjects and topics, can be catalogued and stored. The contents of these files can be helpful in developing and implementing both the resource unit and the lesson plan.

A filing system, for organizing instructional materials and resources, is relatively easy to develop. For example, a survey could be made of the materials and resources available in the classroom, school, and library. Then, a file, based on the findings of this survey, could be set up. The teacher might catalog such items as: maps, magazine articles, news clippings, tables of statistics, cartoons, and pamphlets. This file could consist of index cards referenced to each material or resource identified. Once developed, such a file can be easily kept up to date; and, also, the learners can help to suggest and to obtain new materials.

Instructional Resource Centers and Materials Laboratories. Files of materials and resources should be made easily accessible by being kept in a central location convenient to all teachers. In some school systems, these files could be the responsibility of the central or district office staff. In such cases, the files would constitute a part of the instructional resource center or the materials laboratory. These centers should have a person in charge, and the materials and resources would be available on loan to teachers. This arrangement adds efficiency to the task of identifying, collecting, cataloging, and managing the materials and resources, and can lead to their maximum use. These resource centers and materials laboratories, by their very nature, can serve as coordinating centers for all materials and resources available to the teacher.

Planning the Evaluation Devices

Evaluation is used to determine the extent and nature of each learner's progress toward achieving the instructional objectives. Consequently, the teacher should be concerned that the evaluation devices are meaningful, varied, and have the capability to evaluate all of the objectives contained in the resource unit. The following principles apply to the evaluation process:

Evaluation should be comprehensive. The resource unit should include suggestions of devices for evaluating such learnings as: attitudes, skills, and understandings. Evaluation is not exclusively restricted to the results of paper-and-pencil tests alone. Evaluating a learner's progress, toward the achievement of even one objective, may require the use of more than one evaluation device. Comprehensive evaluation includes such evaluation devices as: standardized achievement tests, anecdotal records, rating scales, aptitude tests, teacher observation, work samples, sociometric devices, activity records, conferences, and role playing.

Evaluation should be coordinated. The evaluation devices should not only flow directly from the objectives of the resource unit, but should, also, be coordinated with the activities and materials as well. Like the other teaching-learning components, the evaluation devices may have to be modified or changed in terms of the requirements of the situation.

Evaluation should be continuous. Evaluation cannot be successfully accomplished if it is conducted only at a terminal point. Instead, evaluation must be a continuous process that occurs throughout the teaching of the unit.

Evaluation should be cooperative. Opportunities should be provided for each learner to assess the extent and nature of his or her own progress, and to, also, participate in the group's evaluation of the resource unit.

Chapter VI
Applying the Resource Unit

This chapter discusses how the resource unit is applied to develop actual teaching-learning situations. For the sake of manageability, each aspect, of the resource unit application process, is described in a separate section. These various sections discuss the application of the resource unit in terms of: (1) the lesson plan, (2) teacher planning, (3) learner-teacher planning, (4) the planning period, (5) the working period, and (6) flexible grouping. However, it should be recognized that the translation of the resource unit into teaching-learning situations is, in reality, a complex, interrelated process.

The Lesson Plan

The lesson plan is drawn directly from the comprehensive compilation of instructional objectives, activities, materials, and evaluation devices found in the resource unit. Several lesson plans could conceivably evolve from one resource unit. Four fundamental ways in which the lesson plan differs, from the resource unit, are discussed below:

(1) The lesson plan calls for much more selective use, in that it is prepared for a particular group of learners.

(2) The lesson plan is more limited in scope, in that it includes suggestions of only those objectives, activities,

materials, and evaluation devices that are appropriate and feasible for the group of learners concerned.

(3) The lesson plan is more precise, in that it contains specific suggestions of teaching-learning components for the total group, small groups, and individual learners.

(4) The lesson plan takes learner-teacher planning into consideration to a degree not necessary in the resource unit, since the latter includes a much greater number of teaching-learning components without particular attention as to how and why they are finally selected for a group of learners.

The teacher, in developing the lesson plan, should give careful consideration to the abilities, interests, and needs of the learners. Also, the teacher must take the amount of time, which can be spent on a particular lesson plan, into account. Thus, the lesson plan may be of long or short duration, depending upon the topic with which it deals; and, also, on the age, grade, and experience of the learners. In addition, provision must be made for articulation, between the preceding and following lesson plans, so as to incorporate logical continuity.

The lesson plan can be applied in two different ways. One way would be for the teacher to write the plan in advance; and, then, to arbitrarily assign it to the learners. A second way would be to develop the plan in advance; and, then, to present it to the learners, so as to enable them to share in the responsibility of planning their actual work. In this way, the lesson plan serves as a reservoir from which the teacher and learners draw suggestions as needed.

The learners' input, into the lesson plan, will probably parallel the teacher's preplanning for the most part. Nevertheless, there will be times when the learners will think of ideas that are not contained in the lesson plan. However, these ideas can be accepted if the teacher and learners become convinced that they are good.

The lesson plan, even though it might have been carefully planned in relation to the resource unit, can be converted into effective teaching-learning situations only through constant evaluation and modification. Thus, the lesson plan must be flexible enough to allow for worthwhile teaching-learning components to be added, and for undesirable components to be deleted or modified.

It is highly unlikely that a lesson plan, once it is used with one group of learners, will be able to be applied, in exactly the same way, to another group, since each group of learners has its own unique qualities. However, successful lesson plans can serve as guides to the teacher in the preparation of similar plans.

The planning process can be greatly accelerated and simplified through the use of an abbreviated lesson plan format. This format, instead of containing word descriptions of instructional objectives, activities, materials, and evaluation devices, simply consists of numbers that are coded to appropriate index cards contained in the resource unit file. In practice, this type of lesson plan serves as a reference for enabling the teacher and learners to pull relevant index cards, containing suggestions of teaching-learning components, from the resource unit file for use in individual and group situations. Moreover, for the sake of convenience, the teacher could compile a master list of the suggestions of teaching-learning components, contained in a given resource unit, for his or her own use in developing and managing the lesson plan.

In computerized unit teaching, the computer retrieves, on the basis of teacher planning and/or learner-teacher planning, suggestions of appropriate teaching-learning components from a resource unit stored in it; and, then, generates a lesson plan. This lesson plan can be in the form of a printout or can be displayed on the video display screen of a desktop microcomputer. However, the suggestions of teaching-learning components, in either format, could best be indicated in statement form. The lesson plan printout and the video display can either be used separately or in combination.

As with the resource unit, the objectives and activities, contained in the lesson plan, can be arranged in random and/or developmental order, depending upon what is to be taught. In the random design, which is particularly applicable to teaching attitudes and understandings, the objectives and activities are selected, on a nonsequential basis, from the resource unit. Thus, the teaching-learning components of the lesson plan, in the random design, are relatively independent of each other.

In the developmental design, which is especially conducive to teaching the basic skills, the objectives and activities are selected, on a sequential basis, from the resource unit. Once implemented, one or more sections, of the resource unit's total sequence of objectives and activities, might be transferred to the lesson plan. There could conceivably be situations in which it would be appropriate for the lesson plan to be designed so that the entire class would be working on the same section of objectives and activities. More than likely, however, different sections, of the resource unit's total sequence of objectives and activities, would be included in the lesson plan in order to meet the widely varying abilities, interests, and needs of the learners. The lesson plan would also probably contain, so as to best accommodate the individual differences of the learners, differentiated sets of consecutively ordered activities for each objective.

The four basic steps, involved in the development of the lesson plan, are set forth in the following sections.

Selecting the Instructional Objectives

The instructional objectives, of the lesson plan, are adopted directly from the resource unit. The objectives:

- serve as the basis for selecting the instructional activities, materials, and evaluation devices;

- provide an overview of the desired attitudes, skills, and understandings to be developed;
- assist the teacher in guiding the learners to develop the ability to generalize, to infer, and to interpret;
- are the focus for continuous evaluation.

The listing of instructional objectives, in the lesson plan, is the teacher's list. These are the objectives which the teacher hopes to see the learners accomplish. However, the teacher can also help the learners to develop their own objectives once the lesson plan is actually applied. These objectives will be of major concern to the learners themeselves. The learners' objectives may differ from those of the teacher in many respects. Therefore, the teacher must, sometimes, be prepared to modify or change the objectives as they are originally stated in the lesson plan.

The number of objectives, in the lesson plan, should be limited to those which are intended to be actually used with the learners. Appropriate objectives are selected for the total class, small groups, and individual learners. In many cases, the same objective will be suitable for both individual and group teaching-learning situations. In addition, it must be determined which affective, cognitive, and psychomotor objectives will be suitable in terms of the learners' abilities, interests, and needs. There may also be instances in which a particular objective can apply to more than one of the three aforementioned categories of objectives.

Selecting the Instructional Activities

The instructional activities, like the objectives, are selected directly from the resource unit. The activities flow logically and sequentially from the objectives, and are interrelated with the materials and evaluation devices as well.

The problem of developing the activities requires that decisions be made about the types of activities which are most likely to achieve the objectives. The teacher, in selecting the activities, must take the abilities, interests, and needs of the learners into consideration. In addition, the teacher should strive to select activities which he or she can suggest to the class as it plans. The class may also have some activities of its own to suggest.

The teacher must consider the relationship of a particular activity to those activities that precede, accompany, or follow it. Although the teacher preplans the lesson plan, it should ultimately be the teacher and learners together who determine the actual activities to be used in teaching-learning situations.

The teacher, in developing the lesson plan, selects appropriate activities, per each objective, in relation to the total class, small groups, and individual learners. As in the case of the instructional objectives, the same activity might be appropriate for both individual and group teaching-learning situations. These consist of whatever introductory, developmental, and culminating activities the teacher considers to be relevant in terms of the learners. This is not to say, however, that a particular activity cannot necessarily fit into more than one of these three categories.

Large group, small group, and individual activities will not all necessarily be designated for each instructional objective. There might also be situations in which the same activity is specified for more than one objective. In addition, it may be necessary to adjust certain activities once the lesson plan is actually implemented. The activities, in the lesson plan, should:

- have the capability to effectively transmit whatever attitudes, skills, and understandings the objectives are concerned with;
- be able to effectively meet the individual characteristics of the learners;
- be designed to enable the learners to actually participate in teaching-learning situations;

• enable the learners to make appropriate and consistent use of such skills as computing, listening, reading, speaking, and writing.

Selecting the Instructional Materials and Resources

The instructional materials and resources, like the objectives and activities, are drawn directly from the resource unit. In the lesson plan, relevant materials and resources should be matched to each activity. Sometimes, the same materials or resources can be used with more than one activity.

Selecting the Evaluation Devices

The evaluation devices, as with the other teaching-learning components, come directly from the resource unit. Evaluation must be a continuous and consistent process, and the lesson plan must be flexible enough to allow for necessary adjustments in the evaluation devices.

Appropriate evaluation devices are matched to each activity. Sometimes, more than one evaluation device is required for a particular activity. Also, there might be cases in which the same evaluation device must be used in conjunction with more than one activity.

Teacher Planning

Teacher planning is a procedure in which the teacher arbitrarily assigns instructional objectives, activities, materials, and evaluation devices to the learners. In this procedure, the learners might not have input even if it should become necessary for the teacher to adjust certain activities once they are actually underway.

It is possible, through the use of teacher planning, to quickly assign teaching-learning components to the learners. On the other hand, teacher planning, because of its usual lack of input from the learners, may fail to effectively provide for the abilities, interests, and needs of the learners. Sometimes, however, the teacher's experience and responsibility may indicate that teacher planning is the most appropriate procedure to use.

Learner-Teacher Planning

Some teachers might plan completely by themselves in applying the resource unit. However, the appropriate use of both teacher planning and learner-teacher planning can usually result in more effective instruction.

Learner-teacher planning is a procedure in which the learners, with guidance, help, and support from the teacher, actually participate in the planning, organization, and evaluation of teaching-learning situations. As the pupils plan with the teacher, they learn to: offer suggestions, make choices, decide responsibilities, respect other viewpoints, and evaluate experiences.

Learner-teacher planning is important from two points of view. First, it contributes to the effectiveness of teaching and learning. The pupils learn better when the purpose of their activity is evident to them. When the pupils plan teaching-learning situations, with their teacher, they know better what it is that they are doing and why they are doing it. Also, the pupils have a better basis for judging whether or not they have succeeded in achieving their objectives.

From the more far-reaching point of view, the learners gain experience, at increasing levels of difficulty, in the instructional planning process itself. They learn how to: define objectives, select activities, choose materials, identify Evaluation devices, and organize for cooperative effort.

Experience has shown that the learners can plan, like to plan, and will work hard to carry out a plan they have made. With very young learners, the plan must be simple and cover periods of relatively short duration with the goals immediately in sight. With older learners, the plan can be more far-reaching, directing the group's activities for several days or even weeks. In such situations, however, a daily review and check-up—"What part of our plan did we carry out today?"—helps to provide the learners with a sense of immediate accomplishment and gives direction to the day's task.

It is characteristic of good learner-teacher planning that:

• the objectives of the planned activities are clearly understood.

• the plan provides something for each individual in the class to do. This is not meant to imply that teachers always work with the total group. They also plan with smaller groups and individuals, but all learners are included in the planning.

• the variety of instructional activities, provided by the plan, is such that each learner can participate in a personally satisfying way.

• the plan has enough flexibility to prevent unexpected events from disrupting the group and making the planning appear futile.

• planning provides for a periodic check-up to measure accomplishment against the lesson plan.

• in setting up a daily schedule, there is enough familiar procedure to give the learner a feeling of security.

• the planning process does not absorb the learners' time unnecessarily. For example, in a classroom where learners are planning what to do in an activity period, as soon as individuals or groups decide on instructional activities, they proceed to do them not waiting for other learners to make their choices.

In general, the appropriate time for planning is whenever a new instructional activity is begun. While each day begins with a plan, it is often desirable during the day to take time to draw the plans for an immediate activity into finer focus. This is not time lost. It gives the closer direction that leads to better use of time.

Teachers have an important part in learner-teacher planning. They must carefully preplan in preparation for the cooperative planning stage. As a result of preplanning, the teacher has many suggestions to make, relative to the instructional objectives and activities, and has a variety of materials and evaluation devices, related to the given topic, ready for class use.

The teacher is responsible, too, for seeing that all the pupils are involved in worthwhile activities, and that each pupil's part in the activity contributes to his or her learning needs. The teacher makes sure that each learner has a balance of activities so that the learner with art ability, for example, does not get all of the drawing assignments, with few opportunities for other experiences. The teacher is respnsible for seeing that appropriate large group, small group, and individual teaching-learning situations are formulated in accordance with the instructional objectives and activities. The teacher uses the plan to keep the learners from straying from their purposes, and to involve the learners in the evaluation of their work.

The Planning Period

During the planning period, the learners and the teacher make cooperative decisions in connection with the teaching-learning components contained in the lesson plan. The teacher might begin the planning period by having the learners ask questions related to the lesson plan. These questions could be initially listed on the board; and, then, transferred to a chart. Next, the teacher might organize the questions under major topics. This list of questions could then be expanded and refined during the course of the planning period.

As the planning period progresses, the teacher encourages the learners to make suggestions concerning what must be done, how it can be accomplished, and how the results can be continuously evaluated. The learners are involved in the planning process as much as possible; but, at times, it may be necessary for the teacher to plan independently of the learners. Also, the teacher should help the learners to realize that not every suggestion can be used.

The teacher helps the learners to select instructional objectives from the lesson plan. Following this, the learners and the teacher select corresponding activities, materials, and evaluation devices in relation to the objectives. Large group, small group, and individual teaching-learning situations are then formed in accordance with these decisions. These cooperatively planned teaching-learning components might not always be the same as the ones contained in the lesson plan, since the requirements of the learners might sometimes necessitate that certain teaching-learning components be added, deleted, or modified. Essentially, the planning period should provide for:

- the participation of all Learners;
- extensive verbal interchange between and among the learners;
- the abilities, interests, and needs of the learners;
- flexibility in developing the plans;
- necessary replanning;
- continuous evaluation.

The Working Period

The planning period and the working period are not really separate and distinct, because planning what to do and doing it actually occur continuously and simultaneously. During the working period, the learners, with the teacher's help, guidance, and support, carry out the previously made plans. The learners, in appropriate large group, small group, and individual teaching-learning situations, are involved in such activities as: doing research, preparing reports, conducting interviews, going on excursions, and performing experiments.

Replanning may be necessary, during the working period, if something interferes with the direction of the work. It is possible that the pupils might have difficulty in carrying out particular learning tasks which were originally planned. If this happens it will be necessary for the learners and the teacher to replan. Such replanning could result in certain teaching-learning components being added, deleted, or modified. Therefore, it is important for the teacher to help the learners to understand the need for occasional replanning.

The teacher must ensure that the learners work on tasks without an undue amount of noise or confusion. To this end, the teacher should:

- be alert to situations in which the learners are confused; and, if necessary, help them to re-establish direction;
- be certain that learning tasks are clear and definite to the learners;
- make sure that all learners have enough learning tasks to keep them occupied for a reasonable period of time;
- maintain continuous contact with all learners by asking questions and making suggestions;
- be certain that the necessary materials are available and that they are distributed in an orderly manner;

• ensure that there is continuous evaluation and replanning.

Flexible Grouping

Within each class there is usually a very wide range in such learner characteristics as: academic achievement, mental aptitude, physical size, and emotional and social development. In view of this, flexible grouping should be used, during both the planning and working periods, in order to better adapt instruction to these kinds of individual characteristics. In flexible grouping, sometimes the total class works together; sometimes it is divided into small groups; and sometimes the learners work individually. However, the teacher, so as to be able to select the most effective grouping arrangement for teaching and learning, must be thoroughly familiar with the characteristics and requirements of the learners.

Flexible grouping should not be regarded as an end in itself; but, rather, as a method to be used in furthering the growth and development of the learners. Grouping is a means of bringing together those learners who share similar characteristics and objectives. It is flexible in that the learners may fit into one group at one time, into another group at another time, and these groups change in accordance with the abilities, interests, and needs of the learners.

The characteristics of the learners determine whatever instructional objectives are selected for and with them. The learners should be organized into appropriate large group or small group situations whenever they share a common objective. Sometimes, however, a particular objective might be identified for only one learner, in which case that learner would work on an individual basis. It should also be emphasized that not all learners will be necessarily working on the same instructional activities in large group and small group situations. For the characteristics, of some or even all of the learners in a particular group, may require the use of differentiated activities.

The three basic types of teaching-learning situations are discussed below:

Large Group Teaching-Learning Situations

Large group teaching-learning situations encourage the learners to share and work in a large social group. Large group instruction can save the teacher much time and effort, because it makes it unnecessary to repeat the same instructional activities with different learners. Some examples of activities that can be used for large group instruction are: viewing a film, engaging in a discussion, going on a field trip, listening to a story, or evaluating and planning the next activities.

Small Group Teaching-Learning Situations

In small group instruction, the teacher adapts the teaching-learning components to the characteristics and objectives of each group of learners. In addition, individualized instruction is provided, within each group as needed, to meet specific abilities, interests, and needs. The learner, by working in a small group situation, may be better able to learn how to: master a particular skill more effectively, learn how to pool information into a committee report, or learn to cooperate in the solution of a group problem.

The role of the teacher, in small group instruction, changes with the situation. At various and appropriate times, the teacher might: instruct the group, or work as a member of the group, or merely observe the group at work. Also, the teacher moves from group to group to provide guidance, help, and support. This enables the teacher to become aware of individual and group abilities, interests, and needs so as to be better able to formulate effective subsequent plans.

Individual Teaching-Learning Situations

The learner works, as an individual, on those instructional activities that apply to an objective designated for only that learner. However, it is conceivable that the learner might also work alone on certain activities in a large group or small group teaching-learning situation. By working as an individual, the learner may be better able to: follow an individual interest, receive help with a problem, or prepare an independent study project.

Chapter VII
Evaluating and Reporting Learner Progress

Evaluation is used to determine the extent and nature of each learner's progress, toward achieving the instructional objectives, and to also identify individual strengths, weaknesses, and problems. Reporting, on the other hand, is used to make learner progress known to parents. Both evaluation and reporting should be an integral part of the unit teaching process, and it is from this frame of reference that this chapter is presented.

Grading

Grading has usually been used to determine and to report the progress of learners. In this system, the teacher first administers a test, either teacher-prepared or standardized; and, then, affixes a numerical value to the result. The testing is usually restricted to an assessment, at stated intervals, of the degree to which the learners have acquired certain facts and skills. Essentially, the learners are tested to determine what they retain, instead of finding out how well they can apply what has been learned.

Grading lends itself to making comparisons between and among learners, and providing, what is on the surface at least, an understandable, if incomplete, method of reporting to parents. Because all learners are measured against a fixed standard, the grades or marks given are sometimes stimulating, but, at other times, are highly discouraging to the learners.

Evaluation

Evaluation, which is much more comprehensive than measurement, is often concerned with interpersonal relationships, attitudes toward work, the ability to do independent work, and organizing and carrying learning tasks to conclusion. A wide variety of instruments have been developed for evaluating aptitudes, academic achievement, emotional development, interests, personal attributes, social development, as well as other phases of the learners' growth and development.

In evaluation, both teacher-prepared and standardized tests may be important, at appropriate times, to measure certain aspects of the learners' progress. However, the emphasis, in the use of any test, is in the achievement level of the individual learner; that is, the comparison of present with previous status rather than comparison with national norms or with other members of the class.

Evaluation is used to promote growth rather than to merely pass judgment. Making judgments are a part of the evaluation process, but such judgments are used to determine the extent and nature of the learners' progress toward achieving the instructional objectives. Evaluation involves not only teachers and learners, but the parents as well. The learners have the need and responsibility to participate in the evaluation of their efforts, and parents and teachers are concerned with the progress of the learners with whom they live and work.

Evaluation, which has diagnostic value, contributes to the teacher's knowledge and understanding of the progress and needs of the learners. Information, obtained through evaluation, is used to help the teacher to adjust or change instructional objectives, activities, materials, and to plan further instruction.

In evaluation, the main emphasis is placed, not on the measurement of accomplishment against a fixed standard to determine growth; but, instead, on the difference between what a learner is doing or can do now, and what that learner did or could do previously. Grades or marks are used, but they are not likely to be numerical ratings, and they have a somewhat different meaning than in the grading system. The teacher uses grades in evaluation to show whether or not the learner is making progress that is satisfactory in light of all that is known about that learner. Thus, a learner may receive a "satisfactory" rating in relation to a particular teaching-learning situation or subject if it is determined that reasonable progress has been made.

Evaluation is used to appraise the effectiveness of the teaching-learning process itself. Such appraisal is concerned with: whether or not the instructional activities are actually bringing about the desired results, whether there is a better way of achieving a particular objective, and whether avoidable mistakes are being made.

Evaluation is periodic in regard to achievement testing, mental aptitude testing, and the like. In most instances, however, evaluation is constant and is an integral part of every teaching-learning situation.

Sometimes, it is necessary for the teacher to evaluate independently of the learners. But it is more desirable, whenever possible, for the teacher and the learners to evaluate both individual and group experiences together, seeking answers to such questions as, "Have we accomplished what we started out to do?" or "What more do we need to know?" Also, the teacher should encourage the learners to evaluate their own efforts independently whenever it is appropriate to do so.

Evaluation is of much value to both the teacher and the learners. The data and information, obtained through the use of standardized tests and other evaluation devices, provide the teacher with insight into the abilities, interests, and needs of individual learners, and the things that they are having difficulty with. Evaluation is used to identify those areas in which the learners need special help, and it, also, provides the basis for a sounder and more informative report to parents than can be provided by periodic tests alone. In addition, evaluation gives the teacher a better basis for judging the effectiveness of the instructional activities and materials.

Evaluation provides direction and motivation to the learners, and helps them to find out what they must do to achieve greater success. Also, the learners have a better basis for satisfaction and are more apt to grow in interest and self-confidence, since evaluation is in terms of each learner's improvement, compared with his or her own previous record, rather than with someone else in the classroom.

Evaluation is a means for improving both the teaching-learning process and the school program. In general, evaluation activities, to be effective, must meet the following criteria:

- The instructional goals and objectives must be clearly established. This includes not only the overall far-reaching goals of the total program, but the immediate objectives of both the learner and the teacher. Effective evaluation can occur only through clearly formulated goals and objectives.
- The beginning point, or base for evaluating the extent and nature of learner progress, must be identified as soon and as accurately as possible. If evaluation is to measure growth, it is first necessary to know "where the pupils are" at the beginning of a new learning experience if progress, as a result of that experience, is to be measured.
- Given clearly defined instructional goals and objectives, and a beginning point, progress is measured, by

both formal and informal methods, by both the learners and the teacher. As a consequence, the evaluation process can be made more stimulating, and can give direction to further effort. Evaluation should be in terms of the individual, and should be made in accordance with his or her unique abilities, interests and needs.

Evaluation can be characterized as being: (1) quantitative and qualitative, (2) continuous, (3) behaviorally-oriented, (4) cooperative, and (5) comprehensive. Each of these five characteristics is discussed below:

Quantitative and Qualitative. Evaluation must be both quantitative and qualitative to be of maximum effectiveness. Quantitative information is provided through such means as tests of academic achievement and mental aptitude. Whereas, qualitative input is related to the evaluation of such behaviors as: the ability to cooperate with others, the expression of ideas and feelings, and standards and values. It is the teacher's task to discover ways for making the subjective assessment of qualitative factors as objective and specific as possible.

Continuous. Evaluation is continuous and concomitant with all other aspects of the unit teaching process; from the initial stages to the final outcomes. Thus, the teacher and the pupils constantly evaluate learning experiences in light of their effectiveness in achieving the instructional objectives. Such evaluation leads to improved teaching and learning.

Evaluation cannot be achieved at a precise time. There is no specific time at which any particular type of evaluation device has more significance than at any other time. Instead, learning behaviors are evaluated on a continuous basis.

Behaviorally-Orientated. The progress of the learners can be best determined if the instructional objectives are stated in terms of behavioral outcomes; what the learner actually does. Objectives, which are defined in terms of desired behavioral changes, point to what is expected of the learners, and the kind of evidence which will indicate whether or not the objectives have been achieved. Essentially, the emphasis is on the acquisition and application of such behaviors as attitudes, skills, and understandings.

Cooperative. Whenever possible, the learners should be allowed to take an active part in evaluation. For, by sharing in the evaluation of their work, the learners are better able to understand the extent and nature of the progress they are making toward achieving the instructional objectives. The learners may be involved in the evaluation of such behaviors as: their reactions to an event observed or participated in, the presentation of reports, the operation of groups or committees, or some accomplishment in relation to the objectives they are seeking to achieve.

In cooperative evaluation, the teacher encourages the learners to appraise their own accomplishments in terms of their purposes. As a result, the pupils learn to become more self-critical and to set standards for themselves. Sometimes, the teacher invites the group to evaluate the work of individual learners. For example, the learners might write stories and then read them to the class. Then, the class could appraise each story, and its reading, in terms of standards which have been previously agreed upon. In this way, the pupils learn, under the teacher's guidance, to become objective and constructive in their criticism.

Comprehensive. Evaluation is comprehensive to the extent that information is collected concerning the learners' emotional, mental, physical, and social growth and development. This means that a wide variety of evaluation devices must be used. These devices are used to: determine needs and interests, appraise potentialities and achievement, provide background for evaluating progress, and appraise group processes. Among the evaluation devices that can be used are: academic achievement tests, diagnostic tests, mental aptitude tests, readiness tests, interest inventories, observational and sociometric devices, and questionnaires.

Other evaluation devices include: anecdotal records, autobiographies, checklists, diaries, interviews, rating scales, and work samples.

The selection of evaluation devices depends upon the particular instructional objective being evaluated. A combination of evaluation devices are often used to determine the extent and nature of learner progress toward achieving a particular objective. Sometimes, however, it is more appropriate to use a single evaluation device to assess progress. In evaluation, the teacher must first determine what kind of information is needed; and, then, must select the most suitable evaluation device(s). Some of these devices have been singled out for consideration in the following paragraphs. These include:

Observation. By carefully observing the learners in a wide variety of instructional situations, the teacher notes progress and identifies continuing and new needs. The learners are observed, as they work in group and individual situations, in order to determine how well they get along with one another, accept responsibility, and make decisions.

Periodic Progress Reports. In this form of evaluation, the learners make periodic written and/or verbal reports which describe the extent and nature of their progress. At the completion of the activities, the learners might also identify how and to what degree their involvement in the activities enabled them to achieve the instructional objectives. In addition, the total group might occasionally be assembled to discuss progress and to share ideas.

Projective Devices. Projective devices can be used to obtain evidence of the learners' behaviors, feelings, and thinking. However, it is essential that the evidence, that is revealed through projective devices, be interpreted in terms of all relevant conditions, data, and factors. The sociogram is one type of projective device, and it indicates the interpersonal relationships that exist between and among learners. The sociodrama is another kind of projective device. With this device, the learners role-play a situation that usually involves the solution of a problem. Other types of projective devices are ones in which the learners are asked to provide an ending for incomplete sentences or unfinished stories.

Tests. The teacher must select and use tests which meet the actual needs of the learners. Standardized tests are used to evaluate such traits as academic achievement and mental aptitude. On the other hand, teacher-made tests are designed to evaluate specific classroom objectives.

Work Samples. The teacher can analyze samples of the learners' work to determine evidence of progress and to identify needs. Work samples could include: committee reports, drawings, outlines, notes taken, and work plans.

Teacher Records. Teacher records are a useful evaluation device. One type of teacher record is a brief running account of any changes or modifications which might have to be made in the instructional objectives, activities, materials, and evaluation devices. Another type of teacher record is a log for individual learners. This log could include teacher notes of such factors as the: interests, remarks, strengths, and weaknesses of the learners. These records can be used to: help and guide the learners, evaluate the extent and nature of learner progress, and report to parents.

Reporting Learner Progress

Periodic reports of learner progress to parents can lead to better cooperation and understanding between parents and teachers. These progress reports are used to provide parents with pertinent information about the learners' academic, emotional, physical, and social growth and development. These reports also specify the learners' needs for help, guidance, and support. Conferences, checklists, evaluative letters, and informal notes are useful devices for reporting and sharing the learners' progress with parents. Each of these reporting devices is discussed below:

Conferences. The progress of the learners can be shared with parents through the use of parent-teacher conferences. Sometimes, parent-teacher-learner conferences can also be helpful. Conferences provide opportunities for: discussing the learners' progress toward achieving the instructional objectives, mutual give and take of ideas, and ensuring that these ideas are clearly communicated. During these conferences, teachers might make use of such devices as: written summary reports, work samples, standardized achievement test scores, and the learners' cumulative records to communicate areas of progress to parents.

Checklists. One type of checklist is one in which each area of learner progress is checked as "excellent," "good," "satisfactory," or "poor," with space provided for the teacher to write comments about each area.

Evaluative Letters. These letters contain teacher statements about learner progress; and, also, provide specific information which clarifies these statements.

Informal Notes. Informal notes, which describe the progress of the learners, can be sent to parents by the teacher. These notes might pertain to such things as: a request for help from the parents, the description of an accomplishment by a learner, or the identification of a particular problem that a learner is encountering.

Chapter VIII
Teacher Education

Teachers cannot expect to make effective use of unit teaching unless they fully understand it. Too often, teachers have conformed to the external aspects of unit teaching without fully grasping its underlying theory, principles, and processes. Therefore, this chapter focuses on how teacher education programs can be designed to help both pre and in-service teachers to develop awareness, knowledge, and understanding of the unit teaching concept and technique.

The Pre-Service Program

It is a familiar maxim that "teachers teach as they were taught." Thus, it is unlikely that teachers will make use of unit teaching if it was not a part of their preparatory experiences.

The Pre-Service Unit Teaching Model

A Pre-Service Unit Teaching Model, for enabling student teachers to understand and to use unit teaching, is presented and discussed in this section. Basically, this model is intended to make it possible for prospective teachers to gain insight into the nature, function, and technique of unit teaching; to acquire the motivation to make use of it; and to develop the necessary skills for actually applying it.

The Pre-Service Unit Teaching model consists of: (1) the introductory phase, (2) the developmental phase, and (3) the culminating phase. Each of these phases is discussed in the following sections:

The Introductory Phase

In the introductory phase, the student teacher is helped to acquire understanding concerning:

- the primary features of unit teaching (what it is, why it is used, and how it is used);
- the psychological aspects of teaching and learning (the nature of the pupil and the learning process);
- unit teaching in relation to: learner-teacher planning, flexible pupil grouping patterns, and individualization of instruction;
- how unit teaching can be effectively used in all subjects at all grade levels;
- how unit teaching can be accelerated and simplified;
- how unit teaching can be used to teach skills as effectively as attitudes and understandings.

The Developmental Phase

The resource unit is emphasized during the first part of the developmental phase. Specifically, the prospective teachers are helped to understand: what a resource unit is, what it is used for, and how it works.

In the second part of the developmental phase, the student teachers do an in-depth study of the resource unit's component parts: the objectives, activities, materials, and evaluation devices. Then, the students, as individuals or in groups, conceive, plan, and construct their own resource units. From time to time, during the development of the resource units, the students come together, as a total group, for the purpose of discussing mutual problems and exchanging ideas. During this phase, the prospective teachers should also be made aware of the need to get into the habit of regularly compiling suggestions of teaching-learning components for all subjects.

The Culminating Phase

The lesson plan is emphasized during the culminating phase. The student teachers study the characteristics and purposes of the lesson plan, and how it is developed from the resource unit. Then, the students formulate their own lesson plans to be ultimately applied in actual teaching-learning situations.

The In-Service Education Program

The above-described Pre-Service Unit Teaching Model can also be used in the in-service education program, if necessary, to enable experienced teachers to develop increased understanding of unit teaching.

Resource Unit Development

Resource unit development is a valuable in-service activity, because it enables teachers to become more knowledgeable concerning: the planning, organization, application, and evaluation of resource units. Furthermore, teachers, by being involved in the construction of units, are more likely to become committed to making use of unit teaching.

The construction of resource units can help teachers to improve both the curriculum and their own teaching. As teachers develop resource units, they can acquire increased understanding concerning:

- the objectives and the overall curriculum of the school;
- the growth, development, and needs of the learners;
- the content items in the various subjects;
- classroom techniques, activities, and evaluation devices;
- available instructional materials and resources.

The resource unit must be carefully developed if its component parts are to be appropriate, relevant, and meaningful. The resource unit developmental process includes the following steps:

(1) determining the topic of the resource unit;
(2) designating the subjects and grade levels for which the resource unit is to be constructed;
(3) identifying the instructional objectives in terms of the attitudes, skills, and understandings to be developed;
(4) determining the instructional activities;
(5) selecting the instructional materials;
(6) identifying devices for evaluating the extent and nature of learner progress.

Resource units may be developed by individual teachers or in cooperation with other teachers. The cooperative approach permits teachers to work together on a common task; and, at the same time, to exchange suggestions of teaching-learning components. These suggestions can be obtained from:

- professional journals, state syllabi, course-of-study outlines, and textbooks;
- the learners themselves;
- resource units;
- systematically recording ideas as they are used;
- attending conferences and visiting other schools.

The cooperative approach also allows teachers to divide the work, and to draw from a wide variety of backgrounds and viewpoints. Teachers, within an individual school, can usually develop resource units very effectively, because they can get together more easily, know the needs and resources of their particular school, and can move more readily from the resource unit to individual lesson plans.

Copies of resource units, whether they be for one classroom, a single grade level, or multiple grade levels, might be kept in either the curriculum library or in a reserved section of the school library. If storage space presents a problem, the resource units' components could be put on microfiche for use with a mechanical viewer. As for computerized resource units, a cathode ray terminal could be installed for enabling teachers to quickly become aware of the contents of the resource units.

The collection might consist of resource units developed by local teachers, professional organizations, teacher education institutions, state education departments, and regional curriculum groups. The teachers would not only borrow from these files, but might, also, contribute new suggestions to them. Instructional materials, which accompany the resource units, could be kept in the same location.

Resource units can never be considered as finished products, because their component parts must be continually adjusted, so as to keep the units useful and up to date. The teacher's observation and evaluation, of the learners' interests and progress, determines the extent to which the components in any particular resource unit need to be modified.

Teachers might maintain an ongoing file of suggestions of teaching-learning components for possible inclusion in current or subsequent resource units. Also, teachers could keep a log of teaching-learning experiences which might include: the success or failure of particular objectives and activities, the degree of the learners' interest and understanding, additional instructional materials which have been identified, and new ideas that have been used successfully. Such information could form the basis for helping the teacher to determine which teaching-learning components to add, delete, or modify in the resource unit.

Supervision

Supervisors should encourage and stimulate all teachers to make use of unit teaching. Nevertheless, teachers are more likely to become committed and enthusiastic if they can use the unit approach on an entirely voluntary basis. For example, supervisors might first identify those teachers who display a genuine interest in unit teaching. Once these teachers have been identified, the supervisor could help them to understand and to apply unit teaching through: providing the teachers with pertinent information; involving them in observing the effective use of unit teaching in actual classroom situations; arranging for the cooperative discussion of results; and developing appropriate follow-up activities. Subsequently, other teachers, as they observe these teachers experiencing success with unit teaching, might then become motivated to want to try it themselves. Supervisory personnel can be of further help to teachers by:

- being supportive of teachers' efforts to make use of unit teaching;
- helping teachers to broaden their experiential backgrounds, knowledge, and skills relative to unit teaching;
- providing teachers with suggestions of resource unit topics;
- helping teachers to develop and refine skills in learner-teacher planning;
- helping teachers to locate instructional materials and to identify community resources;

• organizing a central file of resource units and instructional materials;

• providing opportunities for teachers to observe and to demonstrate unit teaching;

• arranging for in-service education activities in relation to unit teaching;

• helping teachers to anticipate some of the problems that may eventually develop in relation to the use of resource units, and to, also, identify procedures for dealing with these problems when they do actually occur.

The following guidelines can also be useful to supervisors as they work with teachers on unit teaching-orientated in-service education activities:

Guideline I	People work as individuals and as members of groups on problems that are significant to them.
Guideline II	The same people who work on problems formulate goals and plan how they will work.
Guideline III	Many opportunities are developed for people to relate themselves to each other.
Guideline IV	Continuous attention is given to individual and to group problem-solving processes.
Guideline V	An atmosphere is created that is conducive to building mutual respect, support, permissiveness, and creativeness.
Guideline VI	Multiple and rich resources are made available and used.

Guideline VII	The simplest possible means are developed to move through decisions to action.
Guideline VIII	Constant encouragement is present to test and to try ideas and plans in real situations.
Guideline IX	Appraisal is made an integral part of in-service activities.
Guideline X	Continuous attention is given to the interrelationship of different groups.
Guideline XI	The facts of individual differences among members of each group are accepted and utilized.
Guideline XII	Activities are related to pertinent aspects of the current educational, cultural, political, and economic scene.[1]

[1]J. Cecil Parker, "Guidelines for In-Service Education," *In-Service Education for Teachers, Supervisors, and Administrators*. The Fifty-sixth Yearbook of the National Society for the Study of Education, Part I, Chicago: The University of Chicago Press, 1957, pp. 103-128.

Selected Readings

Articles

Arnstine, Donald G., "Programmed Instruction and Unit Teaching," *High School Journal.* Vol. 47, pp. 194-200, February, 1964.

Barrett, Robert E., "Nongraded Learning Units Revamp Junior High School," *NASSP Bulletin.* Vol. 57, pp. 85-91, February, 1973.

Berry, Elizabeth, "The Unit Process," *Educational Forum.* Vol. 27, pp. 357-366, March, 1963.

Blackburn, Jack, "A Learning Activity Approach in Unit Teaching," *High School Journal.* Vol. 47, pp. 201-209, February, 1964.

Burns, Paul C., "A Re-Examination of Aspects of Unit Teaching in the Elementary School," *Peabody Journal of Education.* Vol. 40, pp. 31-39, July, 1962.

Burton, William H., "The Unit Concept in Learning: An Attempt at Simple Explanation," *Educational Outlook.* Vol. 7, pp. 206-213, May, 1933.

Chase, John B., Jr. and James Lee Howard, "Changing Concepts of Unit Teaching," *High School Journal.* Vol. 47, pp. 180-187, February, 1964.

Del Popolo, Joseph A., "A Re-Definition of the Unit," *Peabody Journal of Education.* Vol. 43, pp. 280-284, March, 1966.

Durnin, Richard G., "The Secrets of Successful Unit Planning," *Grade Teacher*. Vol. 83, pp. 92, 167-169, October, 1965.

Ediger, Marlow, "Developing Resource Units," *School and Community*. Vol. 56, pp. 23, 84, November, 1969.

Fitzpatrick, William J., "A Unit Approach for Teaching," *Clearing House*. Vol. 67, p. 352, February, 1963.

Gerhard, Muriel, "How to Write a Unit," *Grade Teacher*. Vol. 84, pp. 123-124, April, 1967.

Godfrey, Lorraine Lunt, "Take a Subject any Subject and Individualize with Learning Stations," *Teacher*. Vol. 91, pp. 59-68, September, 1973.

Harnack, Robert S., "Ten Years Later: Research and Development on Computer Based Resource Units," *Educational Technology*. Vol. 16, pp. 7-13, November, 1976.

Henry, George H., "The Unit Method: The 'New' Logic Meets the 'Old'," *English Journal*. Vol. 56, pp. 401-406, March, 1967.

Kaltsounis, Theodore, "Bridging the Old and the New," *Instructor*. Vol. 80, pp. 54-55, April, 1971.

Kline, Donald F., "Developing Resource Units," *Education*, Vol. 84, pp. 221-225, December, 1963.

Klohr, Paul R., "The Resource Unit in Curriculum Reorganization," *NAASP Bulletin*. Vol. 34, pp. 74-77, May, 1950.

Kniep, Willard M., "Thematic Units: Revitalizing a Trusted Tool," *Clearing House*. Vol. 52, pp. 388-394, April, 1979.

Mannello, George, "Resource Unit Versus Instructional System," *Educational Forum*. Vol. 35, pp. 83-91, November, 1970.

Mickelson, John M., "The Evolving Concept of General Method," *Theory Into Practice.* Vol. 5, pp. 81-86, April, 1966.

Muessig, Raymond H., "Bridging the Gap Between Textbook Teaching and Unit Teaching," *The Social Studies.* Vol. 54, pp. 43-47, February, 1963.

Olmo, Barbara G., "Determining Effective Teaching Techniques in Unit Development," *Social Studies.* Vol. 69, pp. 77-80, March/April, 1978.

Shane, Harold G. and R. Bruce McQuigg, "Unit Teaching and the Integration of Knowledge," *High School Journal.* Vol. 47, pp. 188-193, February, 1964.

Stewart, William J., "How to Successfully Involve Elementary School Pupils in Classroom Decision Making," *Peabody Journal of Education.* Vol. 54, pp. 117-119, January, 1977.

______, William J., "Using the Computer to Improve Unit Teaching," *Journal of Educational Technology Systems.* Vol. 5, pp. 27-32, 1976-1977.

Thompson, Richard A., "Tips on Planning a Reading Unit," *Reading Teacher.* Vol. 27, pp. 156-158, November, 1973.

Veatch, Jeannette, "Individualizing the Social Studies Unit," *Instructor.* Vol. 75, p. 31, November, 1965.

Wagner, Guy, Paul Brimm, and Richard Lattin, "Individualizing Instruction," *Midland Schools.* Vol. 75, pp. 22-24, October, 1960.

Wilson, Gilbert M., "Looking Critically at Unit Teaching," *Instructor.* Vol. 72, pp. 93-94, March, 1963.

Books and Booklets

Anderson, Vernon E., *Principles and Procedures of Curriculum Improvement*. 2nd ed., New York: The Ronald Press, 1965, Chap. 16.

Association for Supervision and Curriculum Development, National Education Association, *Evaluation as Feedback and Guide*. 1967 Yearbook. Washington, D.C.: The Association, 1967.

_________, National Education Association, *Group Planning in Education*. 1945 Yearbook, Washington, D.C.: The Association, 1945.

_________, National Education Association, *Individualizing Instruction*. 1964 Yearbook. Washington, D.C.: The Association, 1964.

_________, National Education Association, *Learning and the Teacher*. 1959 Yearbook. Washington, D.C.: The Association, 1959.

Bloom, Benjamin S., ed., *Taxonomy of Educational Objectives: Cognitive Domain*. New York: David McKay Co., Inc., 1956.

Burton, William H., *The Guidance of Learning Activities*. 2nd ed. New York: Appleton-Century-Crofts, Inc., 1952.

Center for Curriculum Planning, Department of Curriculum, Development and Instructional Media, State University of New York at Buffalo, *Interactive Resource Units for Teachers*. 5th rev., 1978.

De Bernardis, Amo, *The Use of Instructional Materials*. New York: Appleton-Century-Crofts, Inc., 1960.

Dell, Helen Davis, *Individualizing Instruction*. Chicago: Science Research Associates, Inc., 1972.

Faunce, Roland C., and Nelson L. Bossing, *Developing the Core Curriculum*. 2nd ed., Englewood Cliffs, N.J.: Prentice-Hall, Inc., 1958.

Giles, H. H., *Teacher-Pupil Planning*. New York: Harper & Brothers, 1941.

Goodlad, John I., *School, Curriculum, and the Individual*. Waltham, Mass.: Blaisdell Pub. Co., 1966.

Gronlund, Norman E., *Stating Behavioral Objectives for Classroom Instruction*. 2nd ed., New York: Macmillan Pub. Co., 1978.

Gwynn, J. Minor, and John B. Chase, Jr., *Curriculum Principles and Social Trends*. 4th ed., New York: Macmillan Pub. Co., 1969, Chap. 7.

Hanna, Lavone A., Gladys L. Potter, and Robert W. Reynolds, *Dynamic Elementary School Social Studies: Unit Teaching*. 3rd ed., New York: Holt, Rinehart and Winston, Inc. 1973.

Harnack, Robert S., *The Teacher: Decision Maker and Curriculum Planner*. Scranton, Pa.: International Textbook Co., 1968.

Harris, Ben M., and Wailand Bessent, *In-Service Education, A Guide to Better Practice*. Englewood Cliffs, N.J.: Prentice-Hall, Inc., 1969.

Herrick, Virgil E., John I. Goodlad, Frank J. Estvan, and Paul W. Eberman, *The Elementary School*. Englewood Cliffs, N.J.: Prentice-Hall, Inc., 1956.

Jarvis, Oscar T., and Lutian R. Wooton, *The Transitional Elemantary School and its Curriculum*. Dubuque, Iowa: William C. Brown Co. Pub., 1966, Chap. 9.

Kibler, Robert J., Donald J. Cegala, Larry L. Barker, and David T. Miles, *Objectives for Instruction and Evaluation*. Boston: Allyn and Bacon, Inc., 1974.

Krathwohl, David R., Benjamin S. Bloom, and Bertram B. Mesia, *Taxonomy of Educational Objectives: Affective Domain*. New York: David McKay Co., Inc., 1964.

Krug, Edward A., *Curriculum Planning*. 2nd ed., New York: Harper & Brothers, 1957, Chap. 8.

Lee, J. Murray, and Dorris May Lee, *The Child and His Curriculum* 3rd ed., New York: Appleton-Century-Crofts, Inc., 1960, Chap. 7.

Meyer, Edward L., *Developing Instructional Units*. 2nd ed., Dubuque, Iowa: William C. Brown Co. Pub., 1976.

Miel, Alice, and associates, *Cooperative Procedures in Learning*. New York: Bureau of Publications, Teachers College, Columbia University, 1952.

National Society for the Study of Education, *Educational Evaluation: New Roles, New Means*. Part II, Sixty-eighth Yearbook of the Society. Chicago: The University of Chicago Press, 1969.

__________, *In-Service Education of Teachers, Supervisors, and Administrators*. Part I, Fifty-sixth Yearbook of the Society. Chicago: The University of Chicago Press, 1957.

__________, *Learning and Instruction*. Part I, Forty-ninth Yearbook of the Society. Chicago: The University of Chicago Press, 1950.

__________, *The Dynamics of Instructional Groups*. Part II, Fifty-ninth Yearbook of the Society. Chicago, The University of Chicago Press, 1960.

Nerbovig, Marcella H., *Unit Planning: A Model for Curriculum Development*. Worthington, Ohio: Charles A. Jones Pub. Co., 1970.

Noar, Gertrude, *Individualized Instruction: Every Child a Winner*. New York: John Wiley & Sons, Inc., 1972.

Ragan, William B., and Gene D. Shepherd, *Modern Elementary Curriculum*. 4th ed., New York: Holt, Rinehart and Winston, Inc., 1971, Chap. 7.

Saylor, J. Galen, and William M. Alexander, *Curriculum Planning*. New York: Rinehart & Co., Inc., 1954, Chapters 12, 13.

Tanner, Daniel, *Using Behavioral Objectives in the Classroom*. New York: Macmillan Pub. Co., 1972.

Thomas, R. Murray and Shirley M. Thomas, *Individual Differences in the Classroom*. New York: David McKay Company, Inc., 1965.

Van Til, William, Gordon F. Vars, and John H. Lounsbury, *Modern Education for the Junior High School Years*. 2nd ed., Indianapolis: The Bobbs-Merrill Company, Inc., 1967, Chapters 11, 12.

Waskin, Yvonne and Louise Parrish, *Teacher-Pupil Planning for Better Classroom Learning*. New York: Pitman Pub. Corp., 1967.

Wiles, Kimball and John T. Lovell, *Supervision for Better Schools*. 4th ed., Englewood Cliffs, N.J.: Prentice-Hall, Inc., 1975.